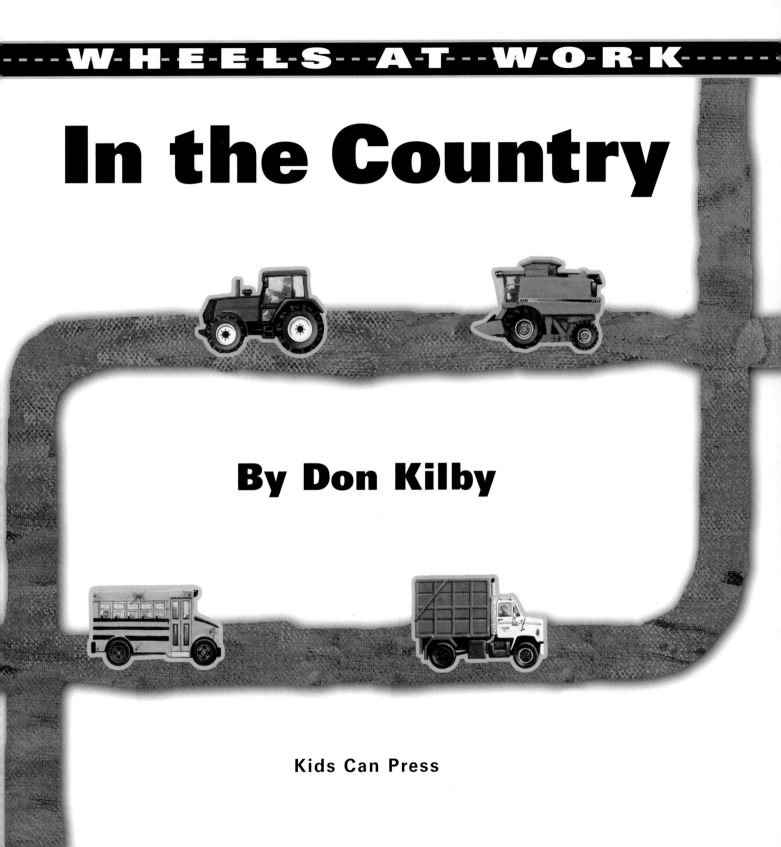

In the Country

By Don Kilby

Kids Can Press

The workday starts early in the country and mighty machines are ready to go! Roll up your sleeves and pitch in as these hardworking machines get to work.

On the farm, trucks handle lots of different chores. After filling up with gas, this **farm truck** will haul a load of feed from the silo to the barn.

The **tractor** is the hardest working machine on the farm. Its main job is to pull all sorts of attachments. In spring, the tractor may tow a seed planter, in summer a baler and in fall a grain buggy. In winter, it can even push a snowblower. Large tires with deep treads dig in and keep the tractor going, even when the ground is rough and muddy.

This eight-wheeled giant is pulling a **cultivator**. Strong metal hooks claw into the soil and break it up. When the field has been tilled, it is ready for spring planting.

The **field sprayer**'s two long arms are covered with nozzles that shower the crops with a fine chemical mist. This protects them from weeds and insects. The driver rides high above the ground so the plants won't be damaged. When the job is done the arms fold in tightly so the machine can travel to the next field.

The **feed mill** supplies farmers with the feed they need for their animals. It's a busy place with trucks rumbling in and out all day long. The mill operator mixes each farmer's special blend from the different feeds stored in the bins and hoppers. Then it's poured into the **feed truck**, which delivers the order.

feed truck

feed mill

Flashing lights at the front and rear of the **school bus** warn other vehicles to stop, so children can get on and off safely.

Children in the country ride the familiar yellow bus to school every day. For some kids the drive is a long one, so there's time to talk with friends or catch up on some homework!

Farm animals are on the move in the huge **livestock trailer** that transports them to and from the farm.

Inside, there are pens on two levels that can hold up to forty cows or one hundred pigs at a time. Holes in the sides of the trailer give the animals plenty of fresh air.

Vast fields of hay are a common sight in the country. When the hay is ready, it is harvested for animal feed. First the hay is cut. Then a **baler** pulled behind a tractor gathers the hay, shapes it into bales and ties them with twine.

It's harvest time! The huge **combine** cuts down the soybean plants and then separates the beans from the stems and leaves.

combine

The beans are blown into a **grain buggy** pulled by a tractor. Everything else is shot out behind. The fields are hot and dusty but inside the combine and tractor cabs it's cool and comfortable.

grain
buggy

In the country, people get their water from wells dug deep into the ground. The **drilling rig** that digs the hole is mounted onto the back of a truck and stands taller than a two-story house! When water starts bubbling out of the ground, the operator knows the hole is deep enough.

"Come on Beauty, step up." A handler gently coaxes the race horse into the **horse trailer**. The trailer is built tall so a horse can stand up comfortably. Inside, the horse will be tethered in a stall, with a hay net full of feed to chew on.

After the crops have been harvested, the fields are fertilized and then plowed to prepare the soil for the next growing season. This tractor is pulling a **plow** that digs six furrows at a time. Each furrow blade bites into the soil, breaking it up and turning it over.

Be on the lookout for mighty machines hard at work next time you're in the country!

To Kookosh

Text and illustrations © 2004 Don Kilby

Kids Can Press acknowledges the financial support of the Government of Ontario, through the Ontario Media Development Corporation's Ontario Book Initiative; the Ontario Arts Council; the Canada Council for the Arts; and the Government of Canada, through the BPIDP, for our publishing activity.

Published in Canada by
Kids Can Press Ltd.
29 Birch Avenue
Toronto, ON M4V 1E2

Published in the U.S. by
Kids Can Press Ltd.
2250 Military Road
Tonawanda, NY 14150

www.kidscanpress.com

The artwork in this book was rendered in acrylic
The text is set in Univers.

Edited by Debbie Rogosin
Designed by Marie Bartholomew
Printed and bound in China

The hardcover edition of this book is smyth sewn casebound.
The paperback edition of this book is limp sewn with a drawn-on cover.

CM 04 0 9 8 7 6 5 4 3 2 1
CM PA 06 0 9 8 7 6 5 4 3 2 1

Library and Archives Canada Cataloguing in Publication

Kilby, Don
In the country / Don Kilby.

(Wheels at work)

ISBN-13: 978-1-55337-472-5 (bound) ISBN-10: 1-55337-472-X (bound)
ISBN-13: 978-1-55337-985-0 (pbk.) ISBN-10: 1-55337-985-3 (pbk.)

1. Agricultural machinery—Juvenile literature.
2. Motor vehicles—Juvenile literature. I. Title. II. Series.

S675.25.K54 2004   j631.3'7   C2003-905840-9

Kids Can Press is a *corus*™ Entertainment company